A Joy

D0546542

# "I Don't Smoke!"

A Guidebook to
Break Your Addiction
to Nicotine

## Joseph R. Cruse, M.D.

Health Communications, Inc.
Deerfield Beach, Florida

*www.hcibooks.com*

The information contained herein is provided for your general information only. This book does not give medical advice or engage in the practice of medicine. Under no circumstances do we recommend a particular treatment for specific individuals. In all cases we recommend that you consult your physician or local treatment center before pursuing any course of drug therapy for nicotine cessation, for example, nicotine replacement therapy.

**Library of Congress Cataloging-in-Publication Data**

Cruse, Joseph R., 1930-
  I don't smoke! : a guidebook to break your addiction to nicotine /
Joseph R. Cruse.
    p. cm.
  ISBN-13: 978-0-7573-1488-9
  ISBN-10: 0-7573-1488-0
  1. Smoking cessation.   2. Nicotine addiction.   I. Title.
HV5740.C78 2009
616.86'506—dc22

                                                                2009025621

Publisher: Health Communications, Inc.
        3201 S.W. 15th Street
        Deerfield Beach, FL 33442–8190

*Cover design by Larissa Hise Henoch*
*Interior design and formatting by Dawn Von Strolley Grove*

### To Sharon

The lady who saved my lungs, and more especially, my heart, for us to enjoy during the third third of my life.

### To Peggy

Special thanks to artist Peggy Musegades for the fun we had doing the illustrations.

*"I DON'T SMOKE!"*

*Most adult cigarette smokers wish they could say that . . .*

*Eighty percent of adult smokers want to quit completely,*

*according to a survey by Gallup and the National Centers*

*for Disease Control and Prevention.*

*But the nicotine in cigarettes is an addictive drug*

*that makes quitting difficult . . . but not impossible.*

# Contents

# Introduction

> *"Hoping is active and wishing is passive.*
> *Hoping means seeing that the outcome you*
> *want is possible and then working for it.*
> *Wishing means just sitting, waiting for a*
> *miracle to happen out of the blue."*

—BERNIE SEIGEL, M.D.

## What This Book Is Not About

This book is not full of depressing statistics on smoking, although some are mentioned. It is not about scaring you with diseases you can get from smoking, although some of those are mentioned. And it's not about shocking you with graphic images of a jarful of tobacco tar or a cancerous lung. Instead, there are some fun drawings.

## What This Book Is About

This book is about a very different approach to smoking cessation. It's an approach that focuses on you—not the nicotine. It's an approach that looks at quitting as a joyous adventure. After all, you're going to be free of a serious addiction—like overthrowing a dictator. It's an approach that will make you laugh and feel good while you are freeing yourself from your addiction. Most important, it's an approach that works. People who have used this program had a high success rate at the end of one year. And they had a good time doing it. They can still say, *"I Don't Smoke!"* So can you.

## Where This Approach Originated

The approach behind *"I Don't Smoke!"* began in 1984 at Onsite Training and Counsulting Counseling, now Onsite Workshops. That year, the company's CEO notified the sixty-five full-time and part-time employees that Onsite staff who used nicotine in any form would be expected to be comfortably nicotine free by November 1985. This would include administrative and clinical staff. Smoking clients were also told that the program and facilities had become smoke free and that an ancillary support program and professional help for nicotine addiction were available to them.

At that time Onsite and many other treatment programs had not seriously addressed the problem of nicotine addiction directly. Other drug problems, including alcoholism, eating disorders, and other mental health problems were more important and seemed to take precedence. Both the public and professional thinking was that the problem was just "smoking," not addiction.

Staff and clients largely accepted the announcement with little disagreement. They knew it was a logical policy, but the smokers were hesitant. They were not happy being caught in the change; the need to stop smoking is scary. But when they took a good look at nicotine dependence as a widespread and powerful addiction with many negative consequences in their lives, their resistance faded.

*"I Don't Smoke!"* is based on the techniques, theories, practices, and procedures that evolved out of that program change and its philosophy. The results were quite encouraging. In addition to everyone pulling together for the "new nonsmoker," the emotional relief and the sharing between smokers and nonsmokers added new dimensions to the program.

Therapists were startled to find that those in nicotine withdrawal were more receptive to therapy than when they were "medicated" with nicotine. The intensity of the work over eight days and the rapid detox with short-term or no nicotine replacement therapy (NRT) allowed most of the participants to return home comfortably free of nicotine. Initial follow-up revealed a 72 percent abstinence rate at the end of one year.

This model for recovery from nicotine addiction is based on increasing self-worth, retraining the addicted brain, use of emotions by receiving help from others, and then helping others. Like any adventure, this model requires action.

HERE IS THE ACTION LIST:
*BELIEVE* YOU ARE WORTH IT.
*CLEAN* HOUSE.
*TRAIN* YOUR BRAIN.
*FEEL* LOVED BY ACCEPTING HELP FROM OTHERS.
FEEL *LOVE* BY GIVING HELP TO OTHERS.

# The adventure starts here . . .

*Don't try to jump over seven-foot bars.*
*I look for one-foot bars I can step over.*

Warren Buffet

This book guides you on an adventure—a true adventure
that will change your life . . .

Many times when an event changes our lives, unless it is
a catastrophe, we are not aware it has changed our lives
until later. We may not be mindful of it at the time. We look
back and say, "Oh yeah, that's when it started to be different . . ." perhaps it was an initial meeting and becoming
acquainted with a coworker. Later the two of you become
important teamworkers.

This is one of those adventures that you will know about *at the time it is occurring,* and it won't be based on a catastrophe. It will be based on a cause for daily celebrating . . . starting on day one!

> THIS BOOK IS WRITTEN TO BE UPBEAT
> AND EXCITING. TO STOP SMOKING
> IS A REALLY BIG DEAL . . .
> YOU ARE SOON GOING TO BE FREE OF NICOTINE!

## The Third Third

This is one book you can judge by the cover. It is a book to guide smokers into the "third third" of their life. That third of life where you can say with pride and gratitude, *"I Don't Smoke!"* The third third of your life can start at any age or at any time. The thirds are not equal. They do not represent actual thirds. They represent the first, second, and third portions of your life. The three portions of your life will vary greatly in duration.

Here is how it works:

1. The years of the first third of your life have come and gone. These were the years in your childhood, and maybe even middle school and high school, when you didn't smoke. This was the initial time you were free from an addiction to nicotine.

2. The second third of your life consists of those years you have used nicotine and continued to smoke even though you may not really want to smoke any longer. This second third ends when you no longer smoke.
3. The third third of your life will be those years when you again don't smoke. This will be the second time you are free from an addiction to nicotine. These will be the years that will span out . . . to become the rest of your life. . . .

Since these are not equal thirds of time, it is an interesting exercise to calculate just how many years each third can contain. For example, let's say that Bill Brown started smoking (secretly, he thought) right after football season ended in his senior year in high school, when he was 17. The first third of Bill's life, the third when he didn't smoke, ended then. Many of his classmates started smoking when they were 13 to 14. For those who started smoking in middle school, or even before, the first third of their lives is shorter than Bill's.

Bill continued smoking through young adulthood and into his thirties and early forties and then stopped at age 42. The second third of his life, his smoking third, ended after 25 years (42 years minus 17 years). Bill lived to be 80 years old, then died of something other than lung cancer. (The odds of dying of cancer of the lung are much greater in smokers, but the odds of Bill dying of cancer of the lung or heart disease after 15-plus years of not smoking are almost the same as if he had never smoked.)

Thus, the third third of Bill's life lasted for 38 years (80 years minus 42 years). Here is a table showing the three thirds of Bill's life. Fill in the table for yourself using today as the age at which you quit. Estimate that you will live to be 80—we hope longer.

| **Bill's and Your Three Portions of Life** (Estimated) | | |
|---|---|---|
| | BILL | YOU |
| First third: | 17 years<br><br>Before smoking | ___ years<br><br>Before smoking |
| Second third: | 25 years<br><br>Smoking | ___ years<br><br>Smoking |
| Third third: | 38 years<br><br>"I don't smoke." | ___ years<br><br>(Estimate) |

THIS BOOK WILL INSTRUCT AND GUIDE YOU,
GENTLY AND SIMPLY, THROUGH THE STEPS
OF BECOMING A NEW NONSMOKER
AND INTO THE THIRD THIRD OF YOUR LIFE.

## Pop Quiz!

Think carefully before answering . . .

1. Are you planning to read this book carefully and slowly so you can absorb practically every word and succeed?

2. Or are you going to read this book carelessly and intermittently because you are just kind of *thinking* that you might quit soon?

3. Are you speed-reading this book because someone gave it to you and they think you should read it?

4. Will you analyze this book and test the author to prove he lacks the special answers that you need? Being a critic would help you forget all about quitting for a little longer, wouldn't it?

5. Addiction recovery requires discipline, directions, and structure. This book provides directions and structure; you need to supply the discipline.

> THIS BOOK IS ABOUT ASKING QUESTIONS
> OF YOURSELF AND GETTING ANSWERS
> FROM—GUESS WHO? YOURSELF!

## Summary

Summary? Why a summary at the beginning of a book? So you can see the big picture before you start . . . and keep your eye on the prize all the way through.

It is important that you understand that the information in this book is not only a complete program, but also one that you can add to with ideas of your own that are fun, helpful, and comfortable for you to use.

You can use this book along with other resources. It can add value to other resources. It can add value to workshops, counseling sessions, personal coaches, group therapy, and Nicotine Anonymous membership. There are many ways to approach the recovery from nicotine addiction. There is a list on the Internet of more than 1,000 "tricks" that individuals have used to quit smoking. This program is designed to be short, intense, and active. And, most of all, permanent.

Let's focus on the active part for now. Remember the action list from a few pages back?

❑ *Believe* you are worth it (stopping smoking).

❑ *Clean* house.

❑ *Train* your brain.

❑ *Feel loved* by accepting help from others.

❑ *Feel love* by giving help to others.


This action list is well grounded in theory and therapeutic models and elements, including:

❑ The importance of self-worth

❑ Addiction theory and brain function

❑ A method to change that function

❑ The importance of our emotions in recovering from addictions

❑ Receiving help and helping others to remain recovered from addictions

This action program has a lot of "to-dos," a lot of busyness. That is what you have this book for . . . to learn to take action. Remember all the drills you did in grade school and high school to master skills and understand subjects? This program has a lot of drills so you can understand and master your brain and profitably use your emotions to stop smoking.

In summary, I hope that you *enjoy* the drills and exercises, and that you find the great emotional uplift, self-satisfaction, and joy as a nonsmoker from day one. Go for it!

# The Table of Contents

The table of contents on pages ix–x lists the important concepts that are the foundation of this program. The concepts are listed in the order that they are best understood, not necessarily in the order of their importance. *All* of the concepts are *important*. To understand these concepts, it is probably best to first read them in the order in which they are presented and then read back and forth for a deeper understanding as you wish.

Chapters 1 through 5 deal with *understanding*. Chapters 6 through 10 deal with the *actions* that are to be taken. *There is a lot of reading and thinking to do before you get to the action part, and smokers can be impatient. Smokers who have decided to stop smoking can be even more impatient.* So here is a little but good exercise to start right now as you read and before you begin the full action part:

*Smoke one, skip the next one, and have a full glass of water . . .*
*Smoke one, skip the next one, and have a full glass of water . . .*

After a day or so, try this:

*Smoke one, skip the next two, and have a full glass of water . . .*
*Smoke one, skip the nextwo, and have a full glass of water . . .*

Since this is a guidebook, it will be used over and over again. You will be asked to perform tasks, keep lists, and write sticky notes and other seemingly silly and serious actions to accomplish the goal of stopping smoking. Take good care of this book, as you will want to review the tasks and checklists now and then. You may even make a diary of brief notes in it. Carry it with you as a reminder of this big project.

Your cheering squad members can be listed in the front of the book. Use one or more of them every day, also.

# CHAPTER 1

# What Are the Barriers to Being a Smoker Today?

*Change is inevitable,*
*except from a*
*vending machine.*

—GOOD STUFF

You've probably heard or experienced most, if not all, of the following messages meant to discourage smoking.

Check each box next to those statements that you know are true or that you have experienced personally:

❑ Smoking is not good for me.

❑ Smoking is an addiction.

❑ Smoking will shorten my life.

**Facts I know:**

❑ Smoking now has a social stigma.

❑ People look down on smokers.

❑ Smoking is not allowed in most places now.

"No Smoking" signs seem to be everywhere now, even in motels. Sometimes the message has a price tag attached:

> WE ASK THAT YOU REFRAIN FROM SMOKING IN YOUR ROOM AND ALL PUBLIC AREAS. A $150.00 CLEANING CHARGE WILL BE APPLIED TO YOUR ACCOUNT TO REMOVE SMOKE ODOR FOUND IN THE ROOM.

A man on a flight from Las Vegas was so controlled by his addiction that he attempted to stuff wet paper towels into an air vent in the restroom while he smoked. He thought it was the smoke detector. After the flight attendant confronted him, he kept an unlit cigarette in his mouth the entire flight. During this time the flight attendant had to keep instructing him to sit down near her seat. She "red carded" him (read him his rights) while the captain kept the seat belt sign on for the duration of the flight. The minute the door was open in Denver, he was arrested, handcuffed, and led off the plane by five FBI agents.

In our society, it appears that cigarettes finally have their backs to the wall...

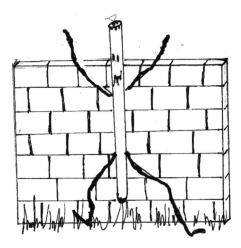

Check each box that applies to you:

☐ I have to go outside to smoke or hang my arm out of sight.

☐ I actually have to sneak a cigarette here or there.

☐ And sometimes lie about it.

☐ I have noticed disgusting stares from strangers.

☐ I need a breath freshener.

☐ I know I smell like smoke—my clothes and hair, my

car, my house . . . even my books and papers.

## Smoking Enablers

Even with all the barriers, warnings, and penalties for smoking, there are still places available that enable you to keep smoking!

***Many businesses are examples of "commercial enablers."***

### Airports

Airports have those glassed-in "opiumlike" dens. The folks inside appear like captured animals. And indeed, they are captured—by nicotine. In the Las Vegas airport, smokers are offered a bank of slot machines in the den to use for their first shot at gambling and a cigarette after the flight—or their last shot at gambling and one more cigarette before the flight.

## Casinos

Restaurants, bars, pubs, and casinos have all lobbied against the passage of antitobacco laws. The sign below is an example of the power of nicotine over commercial institutions. This is an actual homemade sign on the door of a small casino with slot machines and video poker machines. The casino is doing all it can to retain and regain its customers following the passage of new restrictions on tobacco use in public places. The sign said:

---

WE ARE SO SORRY!!!

THIS IS NOW A NONSMOKING GAMING AREA

SMOKING IS NO LONGER ALLOWED INSIDE. WE WANT YOU TO KNOW THAT WE ARE HAPPY TO HOLD THE MACHINE YOU ARE PLAYING WHILE YOU GO OUTSIDE TO THE DESIGNATED SMOKING AREA. WE ARE SORRY FOR THE INCONVENIENCE . . .

NEVADA STATE REGULATION #XX-XXXX

---

In spite of the social pressures directed toward smokers and new laws that enforce penalties with those who break the new smoking laws, these types of commercial institutions have a vested interest in allowing smokers a space apart in which to continue their addiction.

# CHAPTER 2

# What Are My Reasons for Not Smoking?

*When in doubt . . . don't.*
*When there is no doubt . . .*
                    *do it all!*

You probably have a lot of reasons for not smoking. Facing some facts comes first. Read the statements below and check those that ring true for you.

**FACT: You know what it is like to feel . . .**

❑ **Embarrassed,** when someone realizes I smoke.

❑ **Inadequate,** when I have tried to quit . . . and failed.

❑ **Shame,** if someone I love pleads with me to quit and I don't.

❑ **Angry,** when I get pressed about quitting . . . who am I angry at? Them or me or the cigarettes?

❑ **Sad,** when I realize how much money I have spent on cigarettes.

❑ **Afraid,** when I think maybe I can never quit.

❑ **Self-loathing,** because . . . I do smoke . . . I need to take a good look at myself.

Take a good look at yourself . . .

## "*I need to quit.*"

**FACT: Smoking is an addiction to nicotine.**

Nicotine, heroin, methamphetamines, and alcohol all hit similar areas of the brain. They change the brain in ways that result in deep physical and emotional dependency, meaning that discontinuing use is very difficult.

Check the boxes that apply to you:

❑ I don't think of myself as an actual addict.

❑ Because I smoke—and smoking is a full-fledged addiction—I am one. I don't want to be an addict.

❑ I know cigarettes control many minutes, days, and hours of my life and my thoughts . . . it is not fair to me.

❏ How can a chemical like nicotine control me?

❏ I deserve better than being an addict.

## *"I need to quit."*

**FACT: Smoking is dangerous to the health of others.**

Check the statements you believe or have experienced:

❏ I didn't really believe that it could actually hurt others.

❏ I didn't know that family members of smokers are more likely to have trouble with colds, bronchitis, and asthma.

❏ I didn't know that a baby with two smoking parents has inhaled the equivalent of 2,000 cigarettes before he or she is eighteen years old.

❑ I didn't know that "side smoke" (unsmoked cigarette smoke in a room) is more dangerous to others than my exhaled smoke; neither one is good.

❑ I didn't know that a large number of fire deaths in homes are caused by someone smoking (and perhaps drinking) on the couch or in bed.

❑ I have ruined clothes and burned furniture.

## *"I need to quit."*

**FACT: Family, Family, Family . . .**

Check the statements you believe or have experienced:

❑ I really don't know how much worry I have caused my loved ones because I smoke.

❑ My family members have said they don't like my smoking.

❑ My kids might be afraid I'm going to die.

❑ It is hard to talk to the family about my smoking.

❑ Am I afraid they will ask me to quit? (And I can't?)

❑ Do my family members feel that I love cigarettes more than I love them? Good God, do I?!?

# *"I need to quit."*

**FACT: My health could be better . . .**

"My health is probably not as good as it could be . . . even though I feel okay . . . Naturally, I would expect my health and physical functioning to be less than average because I smoke. My physical health has not changed enough for me to give up cigarettes—or has it? I really haven't looked at it . . ."

Check the symptoms you have already experienced or worried about, then add your own:

❏ Chronic cough.

❏ Shortness of breath on exertion, running, playing basketball, climbing, and so on.

❏ Leg cramps and burning with exercise.

❏ Hoarseness, smoker's voice, frequently clearing throat.

❏ Dry skin and signs of aging.

❏ Pucker wrinkles around the mouth.

❏ Loss of singing ability.

❏ Easily fatigued when dancing or working in the house or yard.

❏ Fingers and teeth stained; fingers intolerant to cold.

❏ _____

❏ _____

❏ _____

**Is this how you are feeling?**

"I used to feel pride in my physical condition, but I haven't for a long time . . . I need to get my heart, lungs, muscles, and blood vessels checked . . . I want to be in the best physical health possible for my age and stage . . . If I stop to think about it, I have a lot of living to do . . . "

## *"I need to quit."*

**The Dollar Costs of Smoking Are Serious**

Since you have estimated the three stages of your life using Bill's three stages of life, it should be easy to figure out the costs of smoking. Look at the same table using dollars in place of years. Assume an average use of a pack a day. (Might have been less when you started, more in the middle years, and less in the later years.)

Assume an average pack cost of $2.00 in the first third, $4.00 in the second third, and $5.00 in the third third. Note: the dollars in the third third are dollars saved!

---

### Bill's Estimated Dollar Costs/Savings Due to Smoking/Not Smoking

First third:   17 years ($17 \times 365 \times \$0.00$)  =  $\underline{\$00,000.00}$

Before smoking (no cost)

Second third: 25 years ($25 \times 365 \times \$4.00$) =  $\underline{\$36,500.00}$

Smoking (estimated cost)

Third third:   38 years ($38 \times 365 \times \$5.00$) =  $\underline{\$69,350.00}$

Not smoking (saved!)

## Your Dollar Costs/Savings
## Due to Smoking/Not Smoking

First third:   ___ years = (___× 365 × \$0.00) = <u>\$00,000.00</u>

Before smoking (no cost)

Second third: ___ years = (___× 365 × \$4.00) = \$_____

Smoking (actual cost)

Third third:   ___ years = (___× 365 × \$5.00) = \$_____

*"I Don't Smoke!"* (saved!)

## *"I need to quit."*

# CHAPTER 3

# What Are the Difficulties in Quitting Smoking?

*Avoiding the difficult is a
compelling old habit.
But there is an alternative.*

—MARK WILLIAMS, PH.D.

Most people (95 percent) who use cigarettes *are* addicted to cigarettes. There are people who inhale and can still take or leave it without difficulty; they are called "chippers." Most people (85 percent) who use alcohol are *not* addicted to alcohol. Nicotine is a *strong addiction.*

The average person who quits smoking has tried to quit four to six times previously, so it is not simple; it takes concentration and busyness for a time. That itself is a major barrier to quitting; so are the following.

Cigarettes give the smoker the remarkable ability to get precise fingertip control of the dose of nicotine they need. Achieving the right blood level is the key to almost all drug-induced gratification. Smokers control blood level with ease by how deeply and how rapidly he or she puffs and inhales.

After any period of not smoking, a smoker takes a long, deep puff and blows it out saying, "Aahhh, what a relief . . ." That feeling of relief is not so much a new feeling from the nicotine as it is a feeling of relief from the withdrawal symptoms of the cigarette smoked previously. Plus, there are the perceived good feelings from an old, comforting habit. That long, deep puff is a setup for repeated withdrawals, repeated spells of relief, and then more withdrawal and more relief, and so on. This is chronic addiction.

There are myths about smoking cessation that make it more difficult to quit. It is a myth that the physical withdrawal from nicotine is fierce. It is uncomfortable, but it can *almost* be ignored with patience, perseverance, and preoccupation. It can be like the uncomfortable rock in your shoe when you were a busy kid. You did not want to take time to remove it, and you knew the discomfort wouldn't last forever. It is not a life-threatening process. Many hard drugs are associated with life-threatening withdrawal symptoms, but not nicotine in the form and doses found in cigarettes.

**FACT: Many smokers become so irritated at the pressures to quit that they say, "But I like to smoke!" and for them that outweighs and overshadows the evidence for quitting.**

## My Reasons for Not Quitting

Check the boxes if you believe or have said the following, even to yourself; then add your own:

☐ I don't want to quit. It is one of the few pleasures I have.

❏ I just wish everyone would back off and leave me
   alone.

❏ Maybe I don't give a damn ... (so I keep on smoking).

❏ Everybody I know and like are smokers. If I quit, they
   would probably not care to have me around. (Teen:
   I'm not a nerd/wimp. I can be one of the group. I'm
   as grown-up, tough, and cool as they are ...)

❏ I'm really anxious; I absolutely do not want to gain
   weight.

❏ _____

❏ _____

❏ _____

---

> IF YOU HAVE MORE REASONS
> THAN THIS TO KEEP ON SMOKING,
> YOU PROBABLY WON'T GET
> TO THE END OF THIS BOOK.

---

So, there is a lot going on in a struggling smoker's head.
There are several large "committees" up there and everyone is talking at once. Someone, namely you, needs to get
their attention. Here is what you might be saying that they
listen to. It comes in the form of an addict's inner conversation:

*"This is really strange . . . Usually I feel that I am level-headed, open-minded, and able to make decisions about when and how I will do something . . . but stopping smoking is not one of those things. I can't decide when or how I can do it . . . I don't even know how to start to get started . . . it is as though there is an invisible power holding on to my clothes, not letting me get started or even start to get started! I need a way to start to get started! Can I ever be comfortable, day in and day out, without cigarettes?"*

## *The Answer Is . . . Yes!*

It is possible to be calm and comfortable without tobacco if you understand why and how nicotine has taken over your body, your brain, and your life. Understanding makes it a lot easier to take your life back and be in charge without needing cigarettes or any form of nicotine. It does not need to be difficult. First, you need to learn the following brain stuff.

## Brain Stuff: "I have to have . . ."

*Nurture great thoughts, for you*
*will never go higher than your thoughts.*

—Benjamin Disraeli

There's no question about it, sometimes when you're trying to give up cigarettes, you think, "I've got to have a cigarette, just one." How often do you say or think, "I have to have a cigarette"? Guess what? You don't *have to have* a cigarette; that is your brain talking; your addicted brain—remember? There are things we *have to have*, but nicotine is not one of them:

We *have to have* food.
We *have to have* water.
We *have to have* air.
We *have to have* shelter.

We *have to have* health.

We *have to have* love and connection.

We do not *have to have* nicotine in any way, shape, or form.

*Even in the face of withdrawal symptoms, millions of*
*Americans have conquered their smoking "habit"*
*step-by-step. According to the U.S. government's*
*Agency for Health Care Policy and Research*
*(AHCPR), for every one of the 46 million American*
*smokers, there is an ex-smoker*
*who has successfully quit.*

—Tamar Nordenberg, FDA Consumer Newsletter

## Brain Pathways

Our brains have pathways that serve different functions. These pathways are used over and over again for a variety of functions in and by our bodies. Brand-new pathways can be created, active brain pathways can be dimmed, and old pathways can be reignited. Creating, dimming, and reigniting pathways occurs constantly in the brain thousands of times a second. It is as though the brain is thinking up, forgetting, and remembering at breakneck speeds all day long. Indeed, it is doing just that: 100 billion nerve cells, 100 trillion connections, and the many "feel good" chemicals that are released indicate that our brains can do all of this. Our pathways are formed throughout life as we live our experiences.

Then why does our crazy brain say we *have to have* nicotine?

Each time a nicotine addict (smoker) smokes a cigarette, a pleasure pathway is brightened up. Our pleasure centers are stimulated, and our brain now says, *"Do it again and again and again. Don't stop or I will make you so uncomfortable that you will feel weird things."*

Each time an alcoholic takes in excess alcohol or a heroin addict shoots heroin, their brain sends out the same message, *"This is great! Get me more, more, more! Don't stop or I will send you into withdrawal!"*

The more a person smokes, and the longer a person smokes, the brighter and brighter the "pleasure pathways" become. Nicotine pathways can be dimmed and lose their power when a person stops using the drug nicotine. When they abstain from using it, that person then "recovers" from the addiction for as long as they remain abstinent.

To remain *"turned-on,"* nicotine pathways require steady exposure to nicotine. The timing and amounts required to do this vary among individuals.

*To remain "turned down," addictive pleasure pathways require abstinence.*

Once again, how are these pathways *kept* in a "dimmed" state? By abstinence—not using nicotine in any form. The established pathways of addiction to nicotine undergo major changes during the first *three weeks* of abstinence. It helps to know about these pathways the brain uses as you undertake your smoking cessation adventure.

*New pathways* are created by thoughts, events, behaviors, and emotions.

❑ *Dimming* can occur by forgetting or ignoring a pathway.

❑ *Reigniting* can occur by thoughts, events, behaviors, and emotions.

## Withdrawal Symptoms

Withdrawal symptoms can be quite bothersome. They can be bothersome to you and those close to you! Keep others in mind as symptoms of anxiety, craving, nervousness, preoccupation, loss of concentration, and irritation arise. These are good examples of the many emotional reactions and pain reactions we all might have in other situations. The more attention given to them, the more they bother us. The major symptom is the craving that nags for another cigarette.

**FACT: Withdrawal is a struggle between you and your brain, not you and the cigarette.**

Your brain nags enough to occasionally cause you to shout, "Shut up! Stop nagging me!" And sometimes sadly, "Okay, okay, here is your next fix!" *When you light up, the pathway of relapse brightens up once again.*

Relapse back into the addiction is easy with just a "little" use of the drug (one inhaled cigarette) and everything starts over. This indicates that the original pathways were just dimmed rather than eliminated. They are, therefore, just "lying in wait" and will reignite if exposed once again to nicotine.

Remember, the relief one feels from a cigarette is not due to just a "good" feeling the cigarette gives you directly, but the nicotine is acting like a medication for relief of the withdrawal symptoms your brain is causing.

### How Can *Creating* a Pathway Help?

New experiences and new information constantly create new pathways in our marvelous brain. As we free ourselves from addiction pathways, we need new, strong, *positive* pathways to replace them, a slogan or mantra that says over and over to our brain, *"Hey, I Don't Smoke! Get it? I Don't Smoke!"* Each time that is said, a recovery pathway grows brighter and brighter until it becomes a powerful part of us.

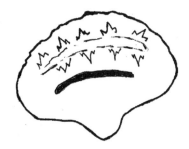

WHEN INFORMATION AND EXPERIENCES
ARE REPEATED OVER AND OVER AGAIN, AND
WHEN THEY ARE IMPACTFUL, INTERESTING, OR
IMPORTANT TO US, WE CREATE STRONG,
POSITIVE PATHWAYS. THEY THEN INFLUENCE
HOW WE THINK, FEEL, AND BEHAVE.

Soon our brain starts "getting clean." We move from the shadow of addiction into easy, comfortable living free of nicotine.

## Smoker's Denial

Remember the reasons for *not* quitting? Those kinds of thoughts require a large amount of denial by the smoker (denial of the truth and of reality). Many addicts suffer from "euphoric recall." They seem to easily remember the good times and forget the bad times. This has been called "nicotine nostalgia" for smokers. It serves as an additional stimulus to continue smoking.

A person who smokes must do a lot of *dimming of their usually helpful* "reality pathways." They must minimize, deny, forget, and debunk any knowledge or awareness they have regarding nicotine addiction. They dim and shut down what they know to be true—that they need to stop smoking.

You must also suppress the feelings that come with being unable to stop a serious addiction, of ignoring the worries of your spouse, children, other family members, and friends.

In smoker's denial, you have to minimize society's intrusion into your being a smoker. In smoker's denial, you cannot truly understand, accept, or feel the need to stop smoking. Therefore, you have no real motivation for stopping. You may say you know you should stop, but you can't feel it to the bottom of your soul. Is your favorite word *but*? *"I know I should quit . . . but . . ."* Addicts are very adept at dimming their *reality pathways*, their *knowledge pathways*, and their *values pathways*. It keeps them in a state of denial where they can continue to justify their behavior.

*To succeed at smoking cessation, people must believe, be motivated, and be committed to conquering their addiction to nicotine.* The fundamental tools for stopping smoking are to brighten up reality, knowledge, and values pathways, while simultaneously dimming the addiction pathway by abstinence. Reality, knowledge, and values pathways are in charge of the recovery from nicotine addiction.

How long does all this take?

Addiction pleasure pathways shut down steadily, dimming a bit each day. Measuring the amount of dimming each day can become a game between you and your brain. You will be able to detect the changes by the third day, and each day you can set a new record.

For nicotine, the craving lessens greatly the first week; the psychological effects lessen within three weeks. Each week becomes easier and more exciting. Actually, the reality of not smoking and the joy of being a nonsmoker starts happening on the very first day . . .

**Hang on! We are almost at the "How-to" part of the book . . .**

# Weird Habits (We Creatures Have . . .)

*Habit is habit, and not to be flung out of the window by any man, but coaxed downstairs a step at a time.*

—Mark Twain

In addition to physical withdrawal symptoms, there are psychological withdrawal symptoms from "habits" developed by smokers. Habits are "programmed" in the brain, but they differ from addictive behavior:

❑ Habits are usually obvious when pointed out.

❑ Habits are more easily changed than addictions (addictions must be recovered from).

❑ Habits can be useful.

❑ Habits are repetitive.

❑ Habits are almost involuntary.

❑ Habits are behaviors that are performed with little forethought of the consequences.

Is smoking an addiction or a habit? It has been called a "bad habit" for years, but smoking is frequently done with little forethought. Many times a day a smoker "just pulls one out," though no special situation is present. Smoking does have a "habit" side to it.

Following are some examples of smokers' accompanying "habits."

Put a check in the box if you recognize your habits,
then add others:

❏ Putting something in your *mouth*.

❏ Having something in your *hand*: the cigarette, a pack,
a lighter.

❏ Having relaxing *rituals* of opening and tapping the
pack and/or the cigarette on the table.

❏ Twirling or rolling the cigarette in your fingers.

❏ Holding the cigarette in different ways.

❏ Frequently looking for smoking people/places.

❏ Checking your supply, making sure you have enough.

❏ Saving partially smoked cigarettes for later.

❏ Ritualistic flipping, tapping ashes, crushing butts.

❏ _____

❏ _____

❏ _____

Old habits are hard to break. Some of the most difficult to break are associated with smoking. They may take as much or more time to change or eliminate than the craving for nicotine itself.

The danger from habits is real. They can serve as powerful "reigniters" (triggers) of the addicted brain's dimmed pathways. How can habits be changed? By awareness and substitution, as explained in later chapters.

# CHAPTER 4

# What Are the Emotional Aspects of Not Smoking?

*Smoking interferes with the
attainment of intimacy and
personal growth. Smoking
serves as a security blanket—
or an insulator from a world of
uncertainty and psychic pain.
It affects our sexual life.*

—SHARON WEGSCHEIDER-CRUSE

## Emotions

In addition to the physical and psychological *withdrawal* that comes with quitting smoking is the *emergence* of an expanded emotional life. This life contains greater joy, greater gratitude, and a greater sense of love than what was available to you during the smoking second third of your life.

Nicotine dulls the emotions, and many cigarettes are smoked just for that purpose—to dull the emotions. It is what we erroneously call "relaxing," when, in fact, we might be avoiding emotions we should be expressing. Emotions are frequently trying to tell us something. That something is not always pleasant or exciting. One very quick and effective way that people medicate emotions is by using nicotine.

Our emotions exist for us to use. They serve us as part of our *sixth sense* for staying safe and enjoying life. Our wonderful five physical senses—sight, hearing, touch, smell, and taste—provide protection from danger and bring us pleasure, beauty, and a connection to others. Our sixth sense does the same. It gives us protection, pleasure, beauty, and a connection to others.

Because our emotions serve as beacons of understanding and behavior toward other individuals, it is important to have them fully available to us. They are there for our use in a healthy way. When someone hurts you or angers you, speak to them rather than smoke at them. For example, good communication between parents and teenagers requires that everyone use their emotions for understanding and guidance. This is important for both the parent and the teenager.

To use our emotions most efficiently as we move into the third third of our lives, we need a few guidelines for emotional honesty:

❑ When we are fearful, we will separate ourselves to protect ourselves.

❑ When we are guilty, we will say, "I'm sorry" and strive to act differently.

❑ When we are hurt, we will talk about it and work to prevent a recurrence.

❑ When we are angry, we will speak out directly without physically acting out.

❑ When we feel happy, we will express it and show it.

❑ When we feel creative, we will set aside a time and a place to create.

❑ When we feel close to someone, we will tell him or her and touch them.

THE MANNER IN WHICH WE USE OUR EMOTIONS
TEACHES OTHERS HOW TO TREAT US.
THEY ARE OUR TRANSMITTED SIGNALS
ABOUT WHAT WE LIKE, DISLIKE, WANT,
AND NEED. OUR EMOTIONS REFLECT
OUR PASSION FOR LIFE.

## Intimacy

We all want intimacy and a life full of passion, especially with another person. Passion and intimacy can be misunderstood. It is more than just physical passion and physical intimacy. *It is the electricity, the spark, the spirit, the "juice," and the living bond between individuals.* It is very fragile and sometimes elusive; it can readily be snuffed out, especially with tobacco. When it is missing, someone might say, "I miss intimacy with my partner." The partner looks befuddled and says, "I don't understand. I feel okay with you . . . close to you. What are you talking about . . . this intimacy . . . what does that mean?"

*Intimacy is the sharing of intense, deep, authentic emotions with another person.* A smoker cannot do this to the fullest. They have feelings that are blunted (dimmed). They have sedated their deepest feelings. They are separated from even knowing what they can feel. If they cannot feel their emotions to their fullest, they cannot share them to their fullest.

It is not to say that smokers do not feel. They do have feelings, but the feelings can be so dimmed by nicotine that they are not clearly felt or understood. There is often an expression of anger, irritation, and impatience. There is a sense of disconnect or incomplete connect in a relationship. There is a big space in it. Nicotine is a sedative; it works by muting important emotions.

## Sexual Feelings

We have the capability to feel passion in many situations, and one of those is sexual. Not only can we feel passionate about music, nature, travel, and learning, we can also feel passionate about another person in a loving, physical, sexual way. When we sedate our emotions, it is very hard to feel full and true passion. We can think passion and get away with it, but we cannot truly share emotional passion when it comes to being a fully present, sexual, sensual person. We become less able to perform sensually and sexually. *Smokers (and drug users) have incomplete and conflicted sexual lives.* With diminished emotional sensuality and passion, it becomes necessary to find sexual arousal and satisfaction in other ways, such as using pornography, violence, excessive masturbation, affairs, and other dangerous, and therefore exciting, behaviors. When we are not capable of a natural, spontaneous response, we find a mechanical, artificial form of stimulation. We then become dependent on what Sharon Wegscheider-Cruse refers to as "mechanical sex." (*Learning to Balance Your Life*, Sharon Wegscheider-Cruse, Health Communications, Inc., 2005. Also on DVD available at www.sharonwcruse.com.)

How do things like seduction and affairs stimulate our emotional sexual life? By providing secrecy, novelty, fear of discovery, excitement, and the promise of instant gratification. When the mechanical sex is over, rather than continued shared intimacy, it usually becomes a shared cigarette, and the opportunity for deep intimacy is quickly snuffed out.

Smokers do have feelings, but for feelings to be most effective, they have to be used accurately and fully. You need to use all your emotions to be the real you. Someone might say they are angry, when underneath they are fearful or lonely. Someone might say they are sad, when underneath they are really angry.

Often someone says how he or she feels just to get by, when in reality they have only dimmed feelings. They are just trying to influence a situation or a person. Diminished, false, and faked feelings rob the nicotine addict of a full emotional life. Nonsmokers who are "shutdown" for other reasons and in other conditions have similar problems with intimacy.

IT IS IMPORTANT THAT OUR
WONDERFUL EMOTIONAL SENSE
IS NOT DIMMED OR TURNED OFF
BY NICOTINE AND OTHER DRUGS.

CHAPTER 5

# What Are the Self-Worth Aspects of Not Smoking?

*To completely stop smoking,*
*and to stay stopped, you must believe:*

> YOU ARE WORTH IT . . . YOU ARE WORTH IT . . .
> YOU ARE WORTH IT . . .
> (THIS IS THE BASIS FOR YOUR ENTIRE PROJECT.)

If you believe that you are an important human being in the universe, that many people benefit from you being here, that just the fact that you were born makes you very special, then you can demonstrate that belief by providing for and protecting your entire self (body, mind, and spirit).

Some people believe that they are "less than." This belief comes from the many "less than" messages that are thrown at us daily. From the time we are children through school and into the workplace, these messages come at us.

To contradict these negative messages, we need to listen to the positive "more than" messages from people who love us, from organizations, from our teachers, and most important, from ourselves. We do this without bragging or strutting. Each day we need to feel that we are worthwhile, worthful, and worth it. . . . We are worth going through whatever it takes to enter and stay in the third third of our lives, where we can say, *"I Don't Smoke!"*

We must believe that we are precious, valuable, lovable, desirable, approachable, respectable, and so on, and so on, and so on. We must have self-worth.

## Messages of Self-Worth that Come from the Inside

If we are not our body, then who are we? Can it be that our brain is not who we really are but is a marvelous organ that can think, sense, and deduct for us? Can it be that the brain is there to guide us, protect us, and help us enjoy the planet? Can it be that the real me is something other than just my brain?

If so, then our brain is just a part of our unique body, a body that was issued to us at the time of our conception. We are inside driving; we are responsible for its safety and maintenance, and as far as we can tell, we only get one chance at it. The fact that we have been given one of these magnificent "machines" requires us to stop in wonder and awe. How has this happened, this "me"? We will quietly wonder this for as long as we are alive.

When a person has a sincere sense of responsibility, when someone believes they and their body are special, when a person is "on guard to guard" their body at all times, they can defeat an addiction to nicotine. They can stop the damaging behavior of breathing in the smoke from a burning piece of paper wrapped around smoldering dried leaves. . . .

WHEN *YOU* BELIEVE AND FEEL
YOUR SPECIALNESS, THEN THAT "YOU" WHO
BELIEVES BECOMES MORE . . . MUCH MORE . . .

None of this has to do with being conceited or being self-centered. You do not need to be self-centered; you need to be a confident, centered self.

One internal source of self-worth and value is remembering what you were like as a child. Almost everyone has a mental picture of himself or herself as a toddler, when the world seemed to dote on them. Perhaps there is an actual photo of the kid you were that warms your heart. Rightly so, this mental image can give you a feeling of worth.

Remembering the most difficult times in your life and how you got through them is another internal source of self-worth. Another is the true love you have for others. We must love ourselves before we can love others. It requires self-worth to have the confidence to take the risk of being vulnerable and available to love others. This amount of self-worth is a powerful stimulus to stop smoking and recover from an addiction to nicotine.

## Messages of Self-Worth That Come from the Outside

Perhaps the most consistent and enduring messages of our worth come from those around us. Family, friends, and coworkers can be a great source of letting us know, in many direct and indirect ways, how valuable we are.

And perhaps it isn't just people that can be a source of self-worth. We all know individuals who feel better about themselves because of the unconditional love bestowed on them by a tail-wagging dog or a purring cat.

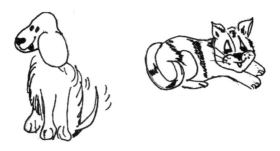

The memories of our accomplishments, as evidenced by plaques on the wall, framed degrees, and letters in scrapbooks, can all give a sense of worth to us years later.

Special occurrences indicate that we must be special. Some examples are opportunities placed in front of us time after time, when we receive commendations, promotions, and raises, and when we celebrate birthdays.

As you now begin the "How Do I . . . ?" sections of this guidebook in the next five chapters, you can incorporate information you have learned in the first five chapters.

*Please read these "How Do I . . . ?" chapters before you start, so you will know what you need to do to set up your program. A summary of the "Twelve Reminders for Recovery" can be found on page 95 for you to use when you have the entire program in mind.*

CHAPTER 6

# How Do I Get Started?

*People who want milk should
not seat themselves on a stool in
the middle of a field hoping that
the cow will back up to them.*

—ELBERT HUBBARD

By far the easiest way to avoid an unpleasant or frightening task is to *not* start at all! Right?

Procrastination is a powerful tool we use to avoid such a task. We put it off until tomorrow; we need to do something else first; we have run out of time; maybe I will fail; and so on. The best way to start is to . . . *start!*

You are beginning that all-important third third of your life . . . remember? This is that part of your life where you, as a person in the third third of your life, can claim sincerely, truthfully, and successfully:

### *"I don't smoke!"*

It is best to start the next steps on a Saturday or Sunday. By Monday morning you will be in a nonsmoking mind-set. During the weekend, it is cleanup time. The first thing in getting started will be cleaning up the residue of years and years of smoking.

During the week and weekend, begin by attending to the following:

*Yourself.* You can begin by cleaning up your clothes, especially woolens. Ask other family members what needs cleaning. If they are not smokers, they will be able to tell you. Speaking of self-care, as soon as possible, schedule a teeth cleaning with your dentist and ask about whiteners.

*The car.* For many smokers, the car can become an ashtray on wheels. Automobile dealers deduct a $250–500 cleanup fee from the trade-in on a smoker's car. Cleaning the upholstery—between and *under* the seats—is important.

*The house.* Then there is the house. Rugs and drapes absorb secondhand smoke readily. Windows and glass cupboards become smoke-covered quite easily, but you may not notice it.

*Other smokers.* You will need to respectfully request that smoking family members and future houseguests smoke outside and provide their own ashtrays. These kinds of negotiations are mentioned in the section on self-care.

*The workplace.* Clean up your desk or work space. Stop in and say good-bye to the salespeople who have sold you cigarettes. And here is a big one: Inform the smokers you usually go on break with what you are doing. You will need to plan different places and perhaps different people to be with for work activities, breaks, and meals.

# Quit Night

***When you wake up the first morning:*** You will have already had six to eight hours of abstinence from nicotine. You quit just before falling asleep. Today you may be facing long periods of enforced smoking cessation, for example, at work. This can result in an easier first day. You probably have been used to going three to four hours without a break. You will need to especially prepare for your breaks without a cigarette. Anticipate those breaks. Breaks can be a trigger!

> **Celebrate! Do not take on the attitude**
> **of a victim or someone deprived.**
> **You are not being deprived**
> **you are being prolonged, right?**

Now the fun begins . . .

1. Go through a ritual of a smoke-scrubbing shower: scrub it off!

2. Shampoo your hair.

3. Brush your teeth.

4. Look in the mirror and say it out loud: *"I Don't Smoke!"* (Check your watch . . . you are starting to train your brain . . .)

# CHAPTER 7

# How Do I Train My Brain?

*Don't limit yourself.*
*Many people limit themselves*
*to what they think they can*
*(cannot) do. You can go*
*as far as your mind lets you.*
*What you believe,*
*you can achieve.*

—MARY KAY ASH

Remember, the person who got up this morning (you), does not smoke. Nope, *that person just does not smoke.* You might even say, "Why in the world do I have this craving?"

## *"I don't smoke!"*

The responsibility for the craving lies with your brain. That brain remembers the effect of that last cigarette you smoked, according to author Allen Carr in *The Easy Way to Stop Smoking*: "You think you smoked it for 'peace.'" But it hasn't given you prolonged peace, because it is disappearing from your body. Your brain is the culprit, the cigarette is its accomplice, and together they are like an alarm clock jangling away. The next cigarette resets the alarm with a temporary fix. This same process can prolong recovery when nicotine replacement therapy is used.

# Keeping Score

The brain is trained by repetition and intensity. If something is repeated over and over to the brain, a new pathway develops and begins to glow. If we practice something over and over again, for example, dancing or quick sprints, our brain sets up a pathway. *When a pathway is lit, our behavior changes.*

A mantra is a Hindu prayer said over and over again until it becomes a part of the person. You can use *"I Don't Smoke!"* as your mantra until it becomes a part of you . . . that is when your behavior changes . . . when you truly *do not smoke.*

## Here Is How to Keep Score in This Tug-of-War with Your Brain

The game is to keep in your head how many times per hour you say, *"I Don't Smoke!"* Be sure to say it every time you think of a cigarette or feel the craving. It will be frequent at first, and then you will see your hourly numbers getting smaller each day.

Those weird craving messages from your brain happen *every six to ten minutes and last for two to six minutes.* The secret is to notice that *they do come and they do go without you doing anything specific.* They pop up less and less each day. Later, even the first day, the frequency of your mantra may decrease. Early on, you may be saying your mantra every six minutes, ten times an hour, maybe more. Keep going, and at the end of every day write down an average for an hour. Just get an estimate. The important part of this is watching the numbers drop. Surprisingly soon, you will find that you are only saying it once or twice an hour.

After four or five days, the fun and the excitement come from noticing those times when you can say, "Hey, I didn't say it once for the past hour!" It is even better when you can say, "Hey, I didn't say it at all this morning!" That starts happening after seven to ten days.

Every time you feel that strange craving in your gut or throat that says "I need a cigarette," answer out loud, *"I Don't Smoke!"* Try to take on an expression of curiosity. If you don't smoke, why in the world would you have this feeling?

If you can, look in a mirror and speak the words. Mirror work can reinforce the message going to the brain. Be conscious of the fact that you are looking at a person—not just an image—that you groom every day.

Also, attach a positive tag phrase onto your *"I Don't Smoke!"* each time you need to say it. For example: *"I Don't Smoke*... good for me!" (Or... "Bless my heart" or... "You are something!")

Here are two more fun brain-training drills:

1. Throw a pack of cigarettes up on your roof. Seriously, do it! If you can't, you may not be really ready for this program. Go ahead—do it! Maybe it will help to get you ready! See if you can do it. (If you find yourself on a ladder before you go to sleep tonight, consider that a sign of a soft, mushy commitment.)

2. Wrap up and sack up your ashtrays in newspapers and a plastic bag. Put them in a neighbor's garbage can. You are less likely to later scrounge through their garbage than your own. Throw out *all* ashtrays.
3. If certain ashtrays have sentimental value, keep them wrapped in a plastic bag and store them for a year. After that, they are nice to use for paper clips and peanuts.

4. Give or throw away your lighters.

*Did you rise to the challenge?* How did it feel? Did these steps have excitement and commitment connected to them? Or anxiety? *Okay, keep going...*

## How Does This Work?

You are not your body. You are not your brain... right? You are somebody special in there. Whoever you are, you live inside your body. Remember, we said that your body was "issued" to you the day you were conceived and it is yours to use all of your life. The organs are there for your use. You are the "boss" of them. For the most part, you tell them what to do. What you do with them determines how healthy they stay and how well you survive in this world. Here are some examples:

❑ When we believe and decide that exercise is good for us, we tell our muscles, bones, joints, heart, and lungs to start jogging or to take a long walk . . . it works.

❏ When we believe and decide that junk foods and excessive sweets make us fat and threaten our heart and blood vessels, we avoid eating them . . . it works.

❏ When we believe and decide that we can move up in our job, we tell our brain and body to work hard, pay attention, create, and learn every day . . . it works.

Of course, many functions of our body, like breathing, heart rate, and digestion are automatic.

> SMOKING IS NOT AUTOMATIC,
> BUT IT ACTS AS THOUGH IT IS.

Can we really tell our brain what to do? Isn't that the opposite of what we have been taught and believe? We are taught that the brain runs the whole show and that we are under the control of it. It bosses us, we don't boss it. Wrong! Except for the "have to haves" mentioned earlier.

> WE CONTROL MUCH OF WHAT
> OUR BRAINS DO EVERY MINUTE.

## The Addicted Brain

Most of our brain activities are very helpful to us, but not the addicted brain's activities. The addicted brain is bossy. In regard to nicotine, our brains tell us what to do ("get more") and what not to do ("don't stop"). Such a brain needs reprogramming so the addiction pathways become dimmed and no longer control us.

When you first stop smoking, the brain quickly informs you it wants nicotine. It is like a spoiled child having a tantrum banging its head on the floor. You need to stay firm and keep telling it, *"I Don't Smoke!"* You can win this tug-of-war with your own brain. You can win it fairly quickly.

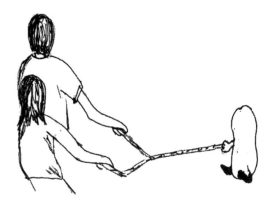

*You* need to be the one in control. *You* have to let your brain know you are in control. *Your* mantra of *"I Don't Smoke!"* repeated over and over gives the brain that message. Your brain and your body will be telling you, "You are in withdrawal."

Your continued abstinence informs the brain that there

won't be any more nicotine coming its way, and dimming of the addiction pathway for nicotine occurs . . . in two-plus weeks comes that glorious day when you realize: "I didn't say my mantra at all yesterday! Hooray!"

## *Winners!*

# CHAPTER 8

# How Do I Use My Emotions?

*Memories, logic, plus
our emotions can provide
us intuition, which might
be our sixth sense.*

—JOSEPH R. CRUSE, M.D.

Suppressed emotions are a much larger part of smoking than people realize. Therefore, some people in their first days as a nonsmoker are surprised by the appearance of anxiety, irritation, and impatience. They feel frustrated.

These emotions are a result of the withdrawal your brain is going through. If your brain is acting like a spoiled little kid, it needs constant caring and consistent discipline, just like a child. You and those around you will need to understand what you and your brain are going through.

> YOUR *PERSISTENCE* AND THEIR
> *PATIENCE* AND *TIME* WILL HELP QUIET
> THE ADDICTION PATHWAYS.

## Use Your Emotions to Increase Your Commitment

How can you enlist the aid of your family, close friends, or coworkers? How can you get them invested in your cessation program? Guess what? They are invested already—they are invested in *you*. They care for you. They want to know how you are breaking your addiction, and they want to know how they can help you.

Your family loves you ... put a sticky note on your bathroom mirror that says, "My family loves me." Put an identical note on your dashboard and on top of the ashtray. If the family is not supportive, use the name of a friend or coworker.

When someone is committed to stop smoking, they need help. Patches, sprays, and gum cannot do it alone. Individuals must have support, whether it is from a formal stop-smoking program, therapists, or from informal support groups such as family, friends, coworkers, the Internet, and Nicotine Anonymous chapters in their community.

There will be people who are *not supportive* of your efforts. They may be smokers not wanting to address their own addiction or they may not want to lose you to non-smoking social groups. This can be true in a family where there is more than one smoker. The importance of negotiating cannot be overstated. Give-and-take is necessary. The issues of a smoke-free house and smoking locations, including the car, need to be addressed. Family members will hopefully agree to attend the family meetings described later. Even smokers can be a part of your cheering squad.

A Phillip Morris study on teenage attitudes and behavior found that kids whose parents smoke are more than twice as likely to smoke (11.1 percent) as kids whose parents don't smoke (4.5 percent). Also, there is a 50 percent reduction in teen smoking when parents sit and discuss the addiction and health problems associated with smoking. Surprisingly, this is true whether or not one or both parents are smokers. (From "Raising Kids Who Don't Smoke" series by Phillip Morris, http://www2.pmusa.com/en/prc/pdf/RKWDS_ Brochure.pdf)

# The Effort Takes Time and Commitment

Your decision to stop smoking is a project that will pre-occupy you and those close to you for a considerable time; everyone is different in their response to it. The time and effort is worth it to all. Everyone can express that fact to one another frequently. They also need to express their per-sonal gratitude that the project is under way. These expres-sions need to be done with happiness and understanding.

Many smokers tend to feel irritable, anxious, and deprived early in their recovery. It is difficult to feel deprived and grateful at the same time. Our emotions are blessings for us to use, especially during times of major change. They help protect us and bring us the joy of accom-plishment.

# Seek Emotional Support from a Group(s)

You cannot be totally alone in this project. Perhaps you have secretly tried to stop smoking alone in the past. For a number of reasons, you have not told anyone of your resolve to quit. (Perhaps fear of failure and embarrassment were too great.)

With each new person who knows about your plan, the person you will become during the third third of your life receives greater and greater commitment to the project. Studies have repeatedly shown that people with a participating family, a group at work, or any good support group are much more successful at becoming smoke free. It is difficult to recover from an addiction in secret. A "chain-smoker" once stated that his resolve to quit smoking got stronger every time he told someone that he was quitting. It worked for him to tell others.

If your family is far removed, use two or three close, agreeable friends or coworkers. (Perhaps people on the same program who are "stopping" like you are.) Most meetings can be brief, but frequent; even a quick stop when passing in the hall. At least once a day there should be a ten- to fifteen-minute meeting during the first three to five days. For a family, this could be just before or after dinner.

## Here Is What the Family/ Group, Club, or Committee Does:

❑ Have an initial meeting face-to-face. Face-to-face is best, especially for families.

❑ Meet daily for the first three to five days, if possible.

Later meetings can be by phone, e-mail, or text messaging.

## Your Meeting Agenda:

1. First, explain your program, show and share this book, and explain the terms and techniques you have learned.
2. Give the group a report on your preparations, struggles, victories, and mantra count. Do this at each contact.

Ask for their feedback, fears, and good wishes—and suggestions.

Some of the meetings of your group need to be longer. There are two "rituals" that can be very significant to all. You may end up going through these rituals several times for different cheering squad members. You may also be able to share in other new nonsmokers' rituals. Just getting the ritual ready is helpful to your cause and increases your commitment to the program.

## The Dear John Letter

You write a letter of good-bye to your cigarettes (see outline on page 71). It should be written as though you are saying good-bye to a lover or dear, dear friend who has betrayed you. Have fun with it. It is true that cigarettes have been friends, companions, and buddies for years; at the same time, they have taken you away from your family and friends. So the example is not as outlandish as it may sound initially. Make the letter as long as you need.

It is helpful to write this letter and make copies for each person you wish to receive it. All these people need not be present. The letter can be mailed to them, and they can be a support person in absentia.

Here is what you do with the letter at the first meeting:

❏ Look each person in the eye and thank them for being one of your supporters.

❏ Remember that you are this new third third person. Say to them, *"I Don't Smoke!"*

❏ Read the letter aloud to the group slowly and clearly so that all can understand.

❏ At the end of the letter is the list of those to whom you will send a copy. Examples are your children, mother, father, best friend in Denver, or whoever is important to you.

# The Dear John Letter

Date:

To:  My cigarettes (nicotine, tobacco, etc.)

Dear Nicotine,

1. Describe how you met, what it was like for you, and how you felt.

2. Describe the good times, what it was like for you, and what you thought.

3. Describe the bad times, what it has been like for you, and how you feel about it.

4. Write "Good-bye!"

_____

(Your name and date)

CC to: Your spouse, partner, daughter(s), son(s), parents, boss, committee, and so on.

## The Death of the Cigarettes

Obtain a double layer of newspaper and spread it out on a table in front of you. Ask your supporters to sit on the other side of the table. Pull out the pack of cigarettes that you didn't throw up on the roof and unwrap them with the usual flair you are used to using. Put the wrapper on the newspaper and open the pack in your own way.

Explain to your supporters that this is the last time you will be opening a pack of cigarettes. Dump all the cigarettes onto the newspaper. Break each cigarette into pieces and tear them apart, mashing the tobacco between your fingers. While you are breaking up the cigarettes, talk about how your life is much better without them and what benefits you expect now in the third third of your life.

## The Funeral Service

When all the cigarettes have been torn apart, the newspaper is carefully folded over the destroyed cigarettes to make a neat little package (a casket!). It is then picked up and held in front of you as you lead a funeral procession around the room.

It helps to have everyone sing the funeral dirge: "da-da-dada-da-dada-dada-dada..." Proceed to a wastebasket or, preferably, outside to a garbage can where the newspaper package of useless cigarettes is dumped without respect or ceremony.

Then, three "hip, hip, hoorays" are shouted out.

Date completed _____

(Several people can participate in this exercise and the Dear John Letter simultaneously, alternating their comments as they go.)

There is a lot to do to get started on this project, and it can be confusing. Once you are off and running, the impact lessens. This is a project that preoccupies you and those close to you for some time. How much time it takes is different for everyone. The time is worth it to all.

Remember, the emotions of abstinence are very important; don't be afraid of them. Quiet music, meditation tapes, and meditation exercises such as yoga and tai chi are great anchors for your day.

The benefits of exercise are extremely important for good health for all of us. Exercise is also a surprising antidote to urgings and cravings, irritability and preoccupation, and anxiety.

Everyone in your groups needs to express their caring, love, and interest in one another frequently.

It is important for you and others to express gratitude that your project is under way. Doing that is helpful. Expressing serious gratitude is often the way to feeling gratitude. Again, it is difficult to be grateful and unhappy at the same time.

Regardless of how you do it, celebrate once a day with somebody who understands what you are doing, somebody who will cheer you on!

> OUR EMOTIONS ARE BLESSINGS
> FOR US TO USE, ESPECIALLY DURING TIMES
> OF MAJOR CHANGE. THEY HELP PROTECT US
> AND BRING US THE JOY OF ACCOMPLISHMENT.

# CHAPTER 9

# How Do I Remain Mindful?

*Mindfulness is not paying more
attention but paying attention
differently and more wisely—
with the whole mind and heart,
using the full resources of the
body and its senses.*

—Jon Kabat-Zinn

The time-consuming part of all this is that it requires almost steady awareness on your part. Your adversary is cunning, baffling, and powerful, just like alcohol or cocaine. We usually go through our days concentrating first on this, and then on that, and time goes by so swiftly we hardly notice it. When we have to concentrate intensely on just one thing, it is as though we are in another world. We forget other things.

We need to *pay attention* to the fact that we don't smoke as we go through a normal, busy day. Our brain might sneak up on us. We have to remain mindful of that fact. There are ways to remain mindful. Advocates of mindful living teach that when we concentrate on the past, or when we concentrate on the future, we miss out on the present. They teach us that quiet times, restful times, and reflection times are a wonderful way to feel present, calm, connected, and confident. It doesn't require a lot of effort or time. to:

STOP! LOOK AT THE SKY, THE TREES,
AND THE FLOWERS . . .

STOP! LISTEN TO THE MUSIC, THE BIRDS,
AND THE VOICES . . .

STOP! FEEL THE BREEZE, THE TOUCH
OF A LOVED ONE . . .

STOP! SMELL FRESH BREAD, PERFUMES,
AND FLOWERS . . .

STOP! SAVOR A TOMATO, A CHIP, A PEPPERMINT . . .

The flight of time is real, the world is real, and we are real. We experience life in the now and in reality. Being aware and living in the present, and therefore mindful, is one of the best defenses against triggers.

## Triggers

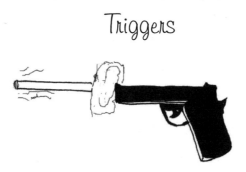

There are many situations and activities that smokers (or anyone who is fighting an addiction) call "triggers." When trigger events occur, people light up without thinking, because having a cigarette is such a routine part of the event. This is especially true if the event is shared with someone else who lights up.

Check the triggers that have caused you to light up, and keep this list available at home and at work so you can guard against getting caught by surprise.

Check the box in front of those situations that are triggers for you:

❏ Cravings

❏ Getting up in the morning

❏ Talking on the phone

❏ Being offered a cigarette

❏ After a meal

❏ A brimming cup of coffee

❏ Studying

❏ Watching TV

❏ Reading

❏ Waiting and waiting around

❏ Being with other smokers

❏ In the john

❏ Leaving a movie theater, bus, airplane, or church

❏ After an argument or an intense discussion

❏ After sex

❏ When tense or anxious

❏ When drinking alcohol

Alcohol and cigarettes go together. In addition, *alcohol can dissolve resolve!* If you can abstain from alcohol during the first month or so of this program, then do it. If you can't abstain from alcohol, think on this:

> INDIVIDUALS WHO HAVE NO TROUBLE
> DRINKING ALCOHOL ALSO HAVE NO TROUBLE
> ABSTAINING FROM IT.
> THEY USE IT AS A BEVERAGE, NOT A DRUG.

## My Other Triggers:

_____

_____

_____

_____

_____

_____

Triggers are stimuli to prompt us into a certain behavior or feeling. Stay mindful of them. Anticipate them, anticipate them, and anticipate them. When a trigger hits or is headed your way (such as a cup of coffee), quickly defuse it with *"I Don't Smoke!"*

## Positive Triggers

Just as there can be negative triggers, we can also have positive triggers in the form of messages that inspire us on our road to kicking tobacco addiction. Many of them can be homemade and personal. Here are some examples:

• Refrigerator notes

• Photographs

"Thanks"

• Sticky notes

• Banners

• Mirror notes

## "You're great"

• Dashboard notes

## "Nice Job!"

• Computer screen savers

• Computer monitor wallpaper

---

HABITS ARE BEHAVIORS
THAT SERVE AS TRIGGERS.
STAY MINDFUL OF THEM.

---

## Mindfulness and Habits

The *American Heritage Dictionary* defines *habit* as: "habit (hab-'it) n. 1.a. A constant, often unconscious inclination to perform an act, acquired through its frequent repetition. 2. an addiction." It is not difficult to understand that our habits can almost subconsciously lead us back into trouble. It is as though the habits that are developed by the smoker are on autopilot and need no thinking to be effective. This makes them even more of a threat. Below are a few habits we listed earlier and suggestions for diminishing their power by substitution or elimination.

## Putting Something in Your Mouth

There is indeed a chance for weight gain when smoking is stopped. Some of this is partly due to a change in metabolism that requires control later on. Much of it is due to using sweets and food as a substitute for a cigarette. The third component is the comfort of having something in your mouth.

All three of these components can be addressed by the use of celery and carrots. Buy baby carrots and stalks of celery. Cut the celery into three-inch lengths. Store them in the refrigerator in water. Keep "traveling packs" in the refrigerator as well. These are for use in the car, at work, and so on (take them to the movies if you can eat them quietly).

Cinnamon, licorice, and mints can occupy your mouth for a time. Get the small size, sugar free. And for a sweet craving, try nonfat, sugar-free instant pudding at bedtime. It is good!

## Having Something in Your Hand

The healing stone of the Lakota Sioux and the state rock of South Dakota is the rose quartz. Small, polished rose quartz pieces are carried in pockets and purses for good luck and for good health. They are smooth, pleasant to the touch, and beautiful to look at. They serve as a conversation piece. It is calming and reassuring when you know that your rose quartz is there to remind you that *you* do *not* smoke. Worry stones are great here, also. Some companies now make them with engravings, using words such as "Love," "Courage," "Serenity," etc.

## Having Relaxing Rituals

Was opening and tapping the pack and/or the cigarette on the table, twirling the cigarette in your fingers, holding the cigarette in different ways, moving, moving, and moving a "relaxing" habit for you? Again, you can use the rose quartz quietly in your hand. You can take several deep breaths to stop the moving urges. Meditation music and other background music are widely available and can be of great help in breaking unwanted urges and cravings.

## Pre-Relapse Habits

There are pre-relapse habits that you should be aware of so that you can intervene on these and eliminate them. They have no value for you; they bring you nothing but threats to your good intentions. If you keep them up, you are in, or close to, relapse. If you catch yourself doing any of the following, especially secretly, call in the mantra! Call a friend or family member and share with them what is happening.

Track the following list, and when these pre-relapse

habits occur, pencil in the latest date they occur and watch that date fade away as you advance as a person who *does not smoke*. Add your own dangerous habits to the end of the list.

_____ Daydreaming about places to smoke

_____ Daydreaming of plans to get cigarettes

_____ Daydreaming or night dreaming about a cigarette

_____ Thinking about getting it smoked

_____ Plotting to get rid of the evidence

_____ Staring at a partially smoked cigarette

_____ Trying to inhale secondhand smoke

_____ Starting to think of reasons to smoke

_____ _____

_____ _____

_____ _____

# CHAPTER 10

# How Do I Build Self-Worth and Practice Self-Care?

*You are always a valuable,*
*worthwhile human being.*

—Dr. Wayne Dyer

We feel good about ourselves for many reasons. One is for what we accomplish; another is for what others tell us about ourselves that is positive. How others behave toward us also tells us much. There is also that small voice inside of us that carries a lot of authority and gives us soothing and scolding messages. Perhaps it is our conscience speaking to us. Perhaps it is direct messages from our values pathway. When our inner thoughts and outer behavior match our value track, the messages are soothing and rewarding. When they don't match, we feel stressed.

Wherever negative messages come from, they sometimes hurt, and a cigarette seems to insulate us a bit. Nicotine addicts are more at risk and have a much more difficult time recovering from their addiction if they do not have high self-worth. If we have had daily hurting messages given to us, we just do not truly believe we are worth saving from nicotine. The truth is that there is hardly a person on earth who isn't worth saving from nicotine.

> HERE'S THE QUESTION IN A NUTSHELL:
> "ARE YOU WORTH IT?"
> HERE'S THE ANSWER IN A NUTSHELL:
> "ABSOLUTELY!"

# Cultivating Messages of Self-Worth

As mentioned earlier in the book, some of our self-worth comes from inside of us while other aspects of our self-worth derive from outside of us. Below are some suggestions to enhance both inside and outside beliefs concerning our self-worth.

## Inside Messages of Self-Worth

Put an "X" on the lines you have completed.

_____ Start the day with *you*; that is, start your morning ritual with a good look at yourself in the mirror. Say "good morning," then, after washing your face and brushing your teeth, look into the mirror and wink—that's right, *wink*! It is amazing how good that feels; a little secret communication between you and you feels good.

_____ Remember a positive phrase tag you want to add to your *"I Don't Smoke!"* tag.

_____ Do someone a favor, but don't get caught. There is something special about being an unnamed angel to someone.

_____ Also, below list three one-line reminders of the most difficult times in your life that you were able to get through and survive. Put a sticky note to mark this page. Whenever you use one of these reminders, think to yourself, *I did it! I made it!* That is good fuel for lighting up a positive emotions pathway in the brain.

_____

_____

_____

\_\_\_\_\_ Cut out some hearts using red construction paper and put the names of loved ones on them. Stash them about so you will be reminded of how much you love and trust them and how much they love and trust you. It takes a lot of self-worth to be aware and grateful of these two facts. You must be worth it—you are stopping smoking!

\_\_\_\_\_ Put a reminder of yourself as a child on the desk, refrigerator, or dashboard (better yet, all three). Do you have a picture of yourself as a kid? If not, there are other reminders of your childhood that will help you see yourself as an innocent child. If you have nothing, make copies of an endearing description of yourself between the ages of three and five.

## Outside Messages of Self-Worth

Put an "X" on the lines next to the statements that characterize things you are currently doing.

_____ Start noticing and enjoying how much physical contact you have with loved ones. Notice how they hang close to you, touch you, and hug you. If it is not enough, then you hang around them, touch them, and hug them. Hugs feel good no matter which direction they travel.

_____ Start noticing and enjoying how much others ask for your opinions, thoughts, and advice. How often do they look to you for predictions and planning?

_____ If you have a pet, stop once a day and spend some time touching, looking at, and talking to him/her. Consider it your daily "feel good together club."

_____ Trek around your house or office or thumb through

a scrapbook and look at those things that attest to your value as an employee, friend, or family member. Look at plaques, certificates, awards, promotions, degrees, commendations, saved letters, and cards. Even though these things may have been within your reach for years, you may have just been walking by without seeing or using them; use them for yourself.

## Beware of the Negative Messengers

You started this project by cleaning up yourself and many smoking-associated "things" in your surroundings. This was done to clear out the distasteful aspects of smoking and diminish the stimuli that might lead you to smoke. The same must be said regarding some of the people in your life. You need to run a checklist regarding "high-risk, high-maintenance" people in your life who cause you stress and/or may be triggers.

Our behavior teaches others how to treat us. We need to behave in a manner that enhances our feeling good about ourselves, not feeling one down. Below is a partial list of characteristics of high-risk, high-maintenance people.

### High-Risk, High-Maintenance Characteristics

Put the initials of each person in your life about whom you have concern next to each corresponding statement.

Once you place initials in front of a characteristic, you will know what to do about that person (confront, and/or avoid, and/or say good-bye, etc.). Add other characteristics to the list.

_____ They do not support your recovery from nicotine.

_____ They offer you cigarettes.

_____ They point out the times you have failed to quit smoking.

_____ They insist you go to smoking environments.

_____ They call you a nerd.

_____ They play the "withdrawal" game. They don't call, stop by, and so on.

_____ They are envious, angry, and critical in many ways.

## Remember: Cheering squads are important!

*Great opportunities to help others seldom come,*
*but small ones surround us every day.*

—Sally Koch

Studies are showing that smoking cessation is most successful when done in a group. The three types of groups that are used to aid those in recovery from nicotine dependency are:

1. Family, twelve-step groups, close friends, and coworkers

2. Self-help discussion groups

3. Professionally led therapy

Some individuals may find it very beneficial to utilize several groups. Find those that best suit you, preferably those who encourage the solutions and do not just rehash the problems. This guidebook has given you guidelines for using motivational, physical, brain training, emotional, and self-worth tactics to help you recover from your addiction. A good support group can continue to offer you all of this. And, surprise! One of the best parts is the feeling of worth and gratitude you receive from helping others.

## Closing Thoughts

Carrying the message of success and gratitude is very exhilarating to the newly recovered person. It seems that the first year is the most threatening for a new nonsmoker just as it is for an alcoholic or other addict. One of the best deterrents to relapse is active participation in getting the word out about recovery. There has not been great emphasis on recovering nicotine addicts personally helping each other over the long haul. The Internet is the exception to that statement, there are hundreds of chat lines, support groups, newsletters, state-sponsored counseling lines, and of course the usual vendors willing to sell. These are fun and very helpful, but there is no substitute for personal contact and sharing. There is a need for volunteering in cessation programs, outreach, and prevention work. Your own success and gratitude can really kick in and grow with you by participation on the cheering squads of others. This is true for family groups, work groups, therapy groups, agency groups, volunteer groups, and Nicotine Anonymous groups. And what if you find there are no ongoing groups near you? The answer to that? Start one!

It is hoped that you feel the adventure and that you are totally and acutely aware that you are changing your life—significantly—as you move into the third portion of your life, the portion where it is a *true declaration of fact* when you say to all of us . . .

## *"I Don't Smoke!"*

# Twelve Reminders for Recovery

1. Clean up the house, the car, and yourself.

2. Start the third third of your life!

3. Wrestle your brain by lighting up values pathways and snuffing addiction pathways (such as *"I Don't Smoke!"*)

4. Gather your tribe (cheering squad) to share feelings.

5. Select a special person with whom to share feelings.

6. Eliminate and substitute new behaviors for smoking habits.

7. Eliminate triggers by avoidance and confrontation.

8. Eliminate dangerous secret thinking by "going public" with your project.

9. Be mindful of your project, your surroundings, and your behavior throughout the day.

10. Love yourself, and express it to yourself daily. Wink and say hello each morning.

11. Express gratitude (past, present, and future) and feel it.

12. Form and join ongoing groups of supporters and become a special person for someone else.

APPENDIX A

# Nicotine Replacement Therapy (NRT)

Medically assisted withdrawal includes "calmer downers," nicotine substitutes, and other medications. Here is a description of the familiar ones. Their actions and possible side effects are given.

## The Options

Most medical aids to smoking cessation are nicotine replacement products. They deliver small, steady doses of nicotine into the body to relieve *some* of the withdrawal symptoms, without the "buzz" that keeps smokers hooked.

Nicotine replacement products are available in four forms: patches, gum, nasal sprays, and inhalers. Like cigarettes, the products deliver nicotine into the bloodstream, but they don't contain the tar and other chemicals that are largely responsible for most of a cigarette's dangerous health consequences. The use of these products prolongs the withdrawal process, as the smoker eventually has to withdraw from the nicotine replacement medication. However, these products can be important for the very heavy smoker or the smoker who has had multiple failures at quitting. It is best that they be used for only the short term. Some of the directions provided by the company suggest much longer periods of use.

## Zyban

The drug Zyban seems to reduce nicotine withdrawal symptoms and the urge to smoke. But Zyban (bupropion hydrochloride), approved by FDA in May 1997, has one thing that sets it apart: It contains no nicotine. It requires a prescription.

Some common side effects from Zyban are dry mouth, difficulty sleeping, shakiness, and skin rash. As many as 3 in 1,000 people taking Zyban may have an allergic reaction, such as itching, rash, and hives, severe enough to require medical attention.

About 1 out of every 1,000 people may have a seizure, which could involve convulsions and loss of consciousness. People should not use Zyban if they have a preexisting seizure condition such as epilepsy or an eating disorder such as anorexia nervosa or bulimia, or if they are taking other medicines containing Zyban's active ingredient, bupropion hydrochloride. These circumstances can increase the chance of a seizure.

Zyban is not recommended for women who are pregnant or breast-feeding.

## Nicotine Patches

Nicotine patches are known generically as the nicotine transdermal system. This method has been available in the United States by prescription since 1992 and in over-the-counter (OTC) form since July 1996. They are sold OTC under the brand names Nicoderm and Nicotrol and by prescription under the names Habitrol and Prostep. Each day a new patch that looks like a big bandage is applied to a different area of dry, clean, hair-free skin and left on for the amount of time recommended in the product's labeling.

A mild itching, burning, or tingling at the site of the patch when it is first applied is normal, but should go away within about an hour. After removing the patch, the skin might be red for up to a day. If the skin develops a rash or becomes swollen or very red, a doctor should be consulted. The patch may not be a good choice for those with skin problems or allergies to adhesive tape.

## Nicotine Gum

The FDA approved Nicorette gum (nicotine polacrilex) for prescription sale in 1984 and began allowing its sale without a prescription in February 1996. Chewing Nicorette releases nicotine into the bloodstream through the lining of the mouth. Unlike gum chewed for pleasure, Nicorette requires a measured routine. It is chewed slowly until a slight tingling occurs or a peppery taste comes out, then placed between the cheek and gum until the taste or tingling is almost gone. The cycle is repeated for about thirty minutes per piece.

Most people find that chewing nine to twelve pieces a day controls their urge to smoke, but the maximum number of pieces that can be safely chewed in a day is between twenty and thirty, depending on the dose of Nicorette. Chewing nicotine gum may not be the right choice for those with temporomandibular joint disease (TMJ) or for those with dentures or other vulnerable dental work.

### Nicotine Inhaler

The FDA approved the Nicotrol nicotine inhalation system for smoking cessation in May 1997. The nicotine enters the user's mouth through a mouthpiece attached to a plastic cartridge. Although the product is called an "inhaler," it does not deliver nicotine to the lungs the way a cigarette does. Almost all of the nicotine travels only as far as the mouth and throat, where it is absorbed through the mucous membranes. Side effects from the inhaler can include cough or throat irritation. Anyone with a bronchospastic disease such as asthma should use it with caution.

### Nicotine Nasal Spray

The FDA approved Nicotrol brand nicotine nasal spray

in March 1996 for prescription sale only. The nicotine is inhaled into the person's nose from a pump bottle and absorbed through the nasal lining into the bloodstream. Nasal and sinus irritation is a common side effect of the nicotine nasal spray. While most people can tolerate the irritation, the spray is not recommended for people with nasal or sinus conditions, allergies, or asthma.

If you decide you want to try one of the four nicotine replacement products, you need to remember the following:

❑ Keep nicotine replacement products, including those that have been used and thrown away, out of reach of children and pets. Even very small amounts of nicotine can cause them serious illness.

❑ Don't smoke, chew tobacco, or use snuff or other nicotine-containing products while using any of the four therapies. It is possible to get an overdose of nicotine. Signs of overdose include headaches, dizziness, upset stomach, vomiting, diarrhea, mental confusion, weakness, or fainting.

❑ Depending on how much you smoked, you may still experience some withdrawal symptoms, or you may feel some side effects from the nicotine, such as headache, nausea, upset stomach, dizziness, or disturbing dreams.

❑ Consult a doctor before beginning any nicotine

replacement therapy, even one that is available over the counter, if you have a medical problem such as heart disease or high blood pressure.

❑ If you take any medications, especially drugs for asthma or depression, speak to your doctor. The dose of a medication may need to be adjusted, because with or without nicotine replacement, the body changes when one stops smoking.

❑ If you are pregnant or breast-feeding, speak to your doctor before trying a nicotine replacement product.

## Chantix

Chantix (varenicline) is a nicotine-blocking agent for which you *must* see your doctor for assessment and approval. It acts as a nicotine-blocking agent and prevents some, but not all, nicotine from reaching the pleasure centers of your brain. It is recommended that Chantix be taken for three months, first in a "loading" dose and then a smaller "maintenance" dose. Just as with nicotine replacement drugs, there are a number of withdrawal symptoms that continue to occur. These can vary among individuals.

The major concern with Chantix is its side effects. These are still under study but can be quite serious. The manufacturer lists nausea, gas, vomiting, insomnia, vivid or unusual dreams, constipation, depressed mood, agitation, changes in behavior, and suicidal thinking or behavior as potential side effects while attempting to quit smoking and taking Chantix. The FDA is requiring manufacturers to put a boxed warning on the prescribing information for the smoking cessation drugs Chantix (varenicline) and Zyban (bupropion)(see page 98). The warning will highlight the risk of serious mental health events, including changes in behavior, depressed mood, hostility, and suicidal thoughts when taking these drugs.

Healthcare professionals who prescribe Chantix and Zyban should monitor their patients for their mental health history and medications and for any unusual changes in mood or behavior after starting Chantix or Zyban. Patients should immediately contact their healthcare professional if they experience such changes. The FAA has banned the use of Chantix for pilots and air traffic controllers. The DOT has recommended that truck driver registrations not be issued for drivers using the medication.

# Resources

Government programs are informational and based on "habit breaking and medical complications." Medical agencies provide suggestions for stopping smoking as well as literature and referral sources.

Programs and information are offered by the following groups as well as many local hospitals and health centers (and there are many more that aren't listed here):

Agency for Health Care Policy and Research
800-358-9295
http://www.ahcpr.gov/

American Heart Association
800-AHA-USA1 (800-242-8721)
www.americanheart.org/

American Cancer Society
800-ACS-2345 (800-227-2345)
http://www.cancer.org/

American Lung Association
800-LUNG-USA (800-586-4872)
http://www.lungusa.org/

American Medical Association
www.ama-assn.org

Centers for Disease Control
www.cdc.gov

Proprietary groups offering programs:
www.mytimetoquit.com
www.quitsmoking.com
www.phillipmorrisusa.com
("Raising Kids Who Do Not Smoke")

Inpatient facilities that have smoking cessation services:
Mayo Clinic
200 First St SW
Rochester, MN 55905
(507) 284-2511
E-mail: stopsmoking@mayo.edu or
call (800) 344-5984

Onsite Workshops
PO Box 250
1044 Old Highway 48N
Cumberland Furnace, TN 37051
Telephone: (800) 341-7432 or (615) 789-6609
E-mail: intake@onsiteworkshops.com
www.onsiteworkshops.com

St. Helena Hospital
10 Woodland Rd
St. Helena, CA 94574
Telephone: (707) 963-3611
(707) 963-6527 TTY/TDD:
Fax: (707) 963-6461
Physician referral phone number: (800) 540-3611
www.sthelenahospital.org

University of Texas, M.D. Anderson Cancer Center
1515 Holcombe Blvd
Houston, TX 77030
(800) 392-1611 (USA)/1-713-792-6161

Hazelden: Your Next Step Program
CR 3, PO Box 11
Center City, MN 55012-0011
(800) 257-7810 or (651) 213-4200
E-mail: info@hazelden.org

www.hazelden.com (see "Frequently Asked Questions")

Fax: (651) 213-4411

## Books

Carr, Allen. *The Easy Way to Stop Smoking.* 1st ed. New York: Stirling, 2005.

Rustin, Terry, M.D. *Quit and Stay Quit: A Personal Program to Stop Smoking.* Center City, MN: Hazelden, 1996.

Wegscheider-Cruse, Sharon. *Learning to Love Yourself.* Deerfield Beach, FL: Health Communications, 1987. See website at www.sharonwcruse.com.

APPENDIX C

# Good News

The following information is from the American Lung Association (http://www.lunguse.org/).

## When Smokers Quit

Within twenty minutes of that last cigarette, the body begins a series of changes that continues for years.

**At twenty minutes after quitting:**

❑ Blood pressure decreases.

❑ Pulse rate drops.

❑ Body temperature of hands and feet increases.

## At eight hours:

❑ Carbon monoxide level in the blood drops to normal.

❑ Oxygen level in the blood increases to normal.

## At twenty-four hours:

❑ Chance of a heart attack decreases.

## At forty-eight hours:

❑ Nerve endings start growing again.

❑ Ability to smell and taste is enhanced.

## The First Year After Quitting

### At two weeks to three months:

❑ Circulation improves.

❑ Walking becomes easier.

❑ Lung function increases.

### At one to nine months:

❑ Coughing, sinus congestion, fatigue, and shortness of breath decreases.

**At one year:**

❑ Excess risk of coronary heart disease is decreased to half that of a smoker.

## Long-Term Benefits of Quitting

**At five years:**

❑ From five to fifteen years after quitting, stroke risk is reduced to that of people who have never smoked.

**At ten years:**

❑ Risk of lung cancer drops to as little as one-half that of continuing smokers.

❑ Risk of cancer of the mouth, throat, esophagus, bladder, kidney, and pancreas decreases.

❑ Risk of ulcer decreases.

**At fifteen years:**

❑ Risk of coronary heart disease is now similar to that of people who have never smoked, and the risk of death returns to nearly the level of people who have never smoked.

# Your Last Task

Please take a moment to e-mail us in the next few weeks or in a month and let us know how you are doing. Your suggestions are welcome! Please send them to: jcruse@idont smoke.net

Additional copies available through www.hcibooks.com, www.idontsmoke.com

# Index

# About the Author

Dr. Joseph Cruse is an oncologist surgeon, an addiction medicine specialist, author, writer, and lecturer. He is the founding medical director of the Betty Ford Center at Eisenhower Medical Center and also served as president of the medical staff at Eisenhower. He served for eight years on the California State Alcohol-Drug Advisory Board and twelve years on the California Medical Association's Impaired Physicians Help Committee. He was medical director for Onsite Workshops, a treatment and training center, for twelve years. Currently, he is a consultant to industry, school systems, hospitals, and alcohol and drug treatment centers.

He has been a guest on *60 Minutes* and *Good Morning America*, and has been featured in magazines in the United States, Australia, and the United Kingdom. His books and pamphlets include *Painful Affairs: Looking for Love Through Addiction, Ripples: A Slogan Story*, and *Family*

*Decathexis,* and he coauthored *Understanding Co-Depen-dency, The Pharmer's Almanac,* and *Experiential Therapy for Co-Dependency.* He lives with his soul mate in Las Vegas, Nevada. They have six children and twelve grandchildren between them.